SCHOLASTIC INC.

Written by Lynda Jones • Designed by Keirsten Geise

Photo Credits: **iStockphoto**: cover: girl detective illustration © aaaniram; page 7: George Washington © Steven Wynn Photography; egg © Donald Erickson; page 8: lightbulb © Floortje; page 9: soda bottles © Jill Chen; page 10: quill and ink © furabolo; page 11: pens © Kaspars Butlers; page 14: tea bags © gaffera; page 15: grapes © Ivars Linards Zolnerovichs; page 17: William Shakespeare © Claudio Divizia; page 18: magnifying glass © Michal Rozanski; page 19: coins © GraĐyna Malek; page 20: checkbook © MBPhoto, Inc., cash © Stefan Klein, ink splatter © stockcam; page 23: digital graphic © Dale Taylor; page 27: fox © Eric Isselée; page 30: books © Soren Pilman; page 31: lipstick © Pali Rao.

Shutterstock: page 4: pen © Swapan; page 9: swabs © fotolibor; page 24: pencils © Jiri Hera.

3DProfi. © Source (RF/CD) via Scholastic Inc: page 26: pen; page 9: lemon; page 17: pen and ink; page 18: heart and ribbon package, love note; page 22: eraser.

Page 6: girl spy © New York Public Library; page 5: Julia Child © Getty images/Hans Namuth; page 17: Abraham Lincoln © Library of Congress; pages 17 and 25: aged paper © CG textures; page 25: pigeon © International Spy Museum. Photography by Keirsten Geise: pages 12 and 13: experiments.

ISBN 978-0-545-59145-4

12 11 10 9 8 7 6 5 4 3 2 1 13 14 15 16
This edition first printing, September 2013
Printed in China 95

TABLE OF CONTENTS

SHHH...

Do you have what it takes to become a supersecret agent? Can you expose hidden evidence like the pros? To find out, you must successfully complete this training mission: Study the case files and master the sleuthing methods in this classified manual.

This training manual comes with a makeup purse. What does it have to do with this mission? It's not what it appears to be. This purse holds a couple of special tools that will help you go undercover. You will learn more about them as we go along.

If you agree to take on this mission, take out the lipstick in your makeup purse. Then use it to sign your name here:

Can't see the letters? Shine the light at the bottom of your lipstick at your signature. See it now? Be sure to use this special pen to pass your message to fellow assets. If someone with sticky fingers nabs the messages and tries to blow your cover, your secret is safe.

REPORT FOR DUTY

This mission is all related to handwriting. It covers invisible writing, forgery, jumbled words, and more. Your training includes exercises on how to comb through clues. You'll learn how to bust bad guys just like the pros. Many of the techniques inside this manual are used by **forensic*** document examiners. These special investigators use cool science to analyze suspicious documents, revealing whether they're genuine or fake.

Before you hit the field, follow these rules:

- Be sure to stay cool and keep your eyes peeled.
- Carry paper to write down observations. (Psst...you'll find a stash inside the box in your makeup purse.)
- Be a good listener (Shh...there's a listening device inside your purse. Bob your head while wearing it. People will think that you're listening to music instead of eavesdropping.)
- Do not reveal your secret identity! See master agent below.

In the 1960s, Julia Child became a famous TV chef and cookbook author. Few people back then suspected this: During World War II in the 1940s, she worked for the government agency that is now known as the Central Intelligence Agency.

*Words in bold are defined in the glossary on page 32.

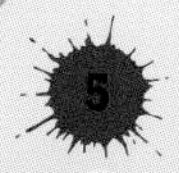

Historic Heroines
This drawing from 1782 shows a "girl agent" sneaking supplies to a fort during the Revolutionary War.

CASE NO. 1: Petticoat Patriots

These daredevils used sneaky ways to communicate with their contacts.

During the Revolutionary War (1775–1783), America fought for independence from Britain. Many women took part in the war effort by serving as secret agents. Some volunteered and others were recruited by General George Washington's army. Their mission: to snoop on British troops.

The soldiers thought that women were too clueless to understand military strategies, so they openly discussed top secret plans in front of them. Little did they know that these lady agents had the know-how to sabotage their plans!

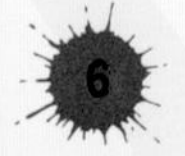

When the agents learned details about the enemy's movements, they sent messages, warning General Washington. Sometimes, the messages were written in invisible ink. The hidden dispatches were revealed by using heat or chemicals.

General George Washington

Head Honcho

After leading America to victory, George Washington served as the first president of the United States from 1789 to 1797. He was the only U.S. president who was unanimously elected.

TRADE SECRETS FROM THE HIDDEN FILES

Secret meeting at noon.

Shhh Giovanni Porta, a 16th-century Italian scientist, discovered a way to hide secret messages inside eggs. Porta created an ink made of vinegar and the chemical alum. Then he used the ink to write on the shell of a hard-boiled egg. The ink seeped through the egg's **porous** shell, leaving no trace on the surface. But the ink stained the boiled egg white inside. To read the message, the recipient removed the shell.

Training Exercise:
Ink a Secret Message

Just like the early agents, you must be able to pass notes undetected. Learn how to make invisible ink.

You Need:

- ☑ Lemon juice or juice of 1 lemon
- ☑ Small bowl
- ☑ Piece of unlined white paper
- ☑ Cotton swab
- ☑ Lamp
- ☑ Senior agent (adult helper)

To Do:

1. Put lemon juice into a small bowl.
2. Dip cotton swab into the lemon juice.
3. Write a secret message on a piece of paper. Let it dry completely.
4. Ask a senior agent to hold the paper over a warm lightbulb.
5. Watch what develops.

ALERT

If the lamp is too hot, the paper will burn. Never use halogen lightbulbs for this activity. The bulbs are superhot.

TRADE SECRETS REVEALED

Lemon juice contains citric **acid**. When you hold the paper over the lightbulb, heat causes the acid to break down. The remaining material in the lemon juice **oxidizes** and turns brown, revealing the hidden message.

TRADE SECRETS FROM THE HIDDEN FILES

Shhh

Any acidic fluid can be used as invisible ink that appears using heat. That includes vinegar, milk, fruit juices, and soda pop. During World War II, secret agents often used their own saliva or urine to make invisible ink.

CASE NO. 2:

Operation Bullpen

Autograph Forgers—BUSTED!

In the 1990s, a group of scam artists forged the signatures of athletes and historical figures. The crooks' work was so masterful they fooled many experts into thinking that they were real. One trick the forgers used to make the autographs look convincing as antique: They used inks and paper that were made during the era when the forged individual was alive.

The scoundrels sold the loot online, in shops, and even on TV home-shopping channels. The sudden flood of autographs in the market made the FBI question: Antique signatures were rarely for sale a decade ago, so where did the bounty come from?

Detectives tailed the forgers, who were reaping sales up to $100 million! The agents of "Operation Bullpen" eventually gathered enough evidence to bust the scam.

Training Exercise: Chromatography

If you want to stop forgers, you need to be a pro at **chromatography**. This technique helps you identify the inks used in documents.

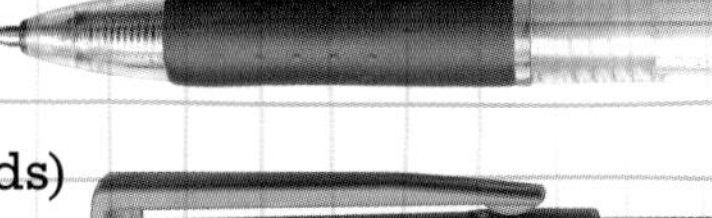

You Need:

- ☑ Fellow agent
- ☑ Sheet of white paper
- ☑ 2 black pens (different brands)
- ☑ 2 blue pens (different brands)
- ☑ Toothpick
- ☑ Clear tape
- ☑ Small container with lid
- ☑ Straw
- ☑ Paper towel
- ☑ Rubbing alcohol
- ☑ 8 strips of chromatography paper*

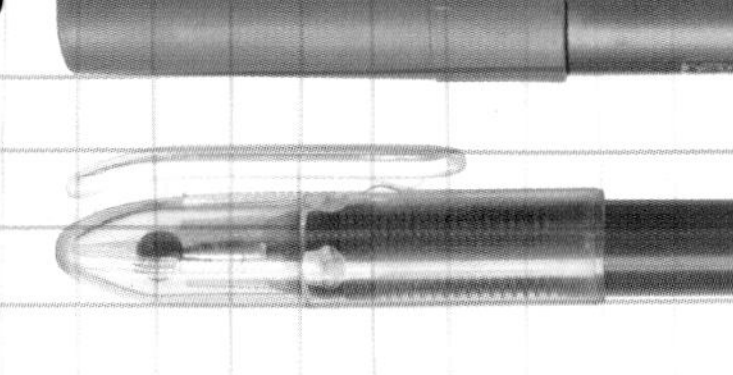

Have an adult help perform the steps involving rubbing alcohol. Be sure to study the warning label on the alcohol bottle.

*To make chromatography paper, cut a white coffee filter into strips each measuring 2.5 in. X 0.5 in. (6.4 cm X 1.3 cm).

To Do:

1. Assign a letter to each pen: A, B, C, and D.
2. Have a fellow agent select one of the four pens (without telling you which one) and write this on a piece of paper: "Shh . . . I'll meet you at the mall."

step 6

3. Use pen A to make a dot about 1 in. (2.5 cm) from the bottom of a strip of chromatography paper.
4. Tape the top of the strip to the center of the toothpick.
5. Position the toothpick across the rim of the container, hanging the paper strip in the center.
6. Fill the container with enough water so that only the tip of the paper touches the water.
7. Allow the water to rise up the paper. When the water reaches the ink dot, the liquid will continue rising with or without some of the ink.
8. When the ink stops rising, remove the paper and place it on a paper towel.
9. Repeat Steps 3 to 8 for each of pens B, C, and D.
10. If the ink in some of your pens was not **soluble** in water (ink did not spread), use those pens to repeat Steps 3 to 8. This time, fill the container with rubbing alcohol instead of water.
11. Cut a piece of the agent's writing and put it on the container's lid.

12. Add several drops of water onto the writing. Wait several minutes to see if the ink is soluble in water. If not, repeat Steps 11 and 12 using alcohol.
13. Dip the end of a straw into the ink solution on the lid. Transfer the ink onto a blank piece of chromatography paper, about an inch from the bottom.
14. Test the strip using Steps 4 to 8. Be sure to use the correct **solvent**.
15. Compare the result with those from the four pens. Find the match.

TRADE SECRETS REVEALED

All inks contain a unique formula of color **pigments**. When the solvent hits the ink spot, it causes the pigments in the ink to separate according to the size of their molecules. Smaller pigment molecules travel quickly up the paper. Larger pigment molecules move slower and remain at the bottom. The resulting image on the paper is a **chromatogram**, which shows all the various pigments present in one ink sample. Different brands of pens produce different chromatograms.

Training Exercise: Aging Paper

Old paper is brown and delicate. The crooks who were nabbed by Operation Bullpen ripped blank pages from vintage books and used them for forgery. Less sneaky crooks might use this method to give new paper an aged look.

You Need:

- ☑ 3 tea bags of black tea
- ☑ 2 cups of warm water
- ☑ Large bowl
- ☑ White bond or cardstock paper
- ☑ Pen
- ☑ Tray
- ☑ Paper towels
- ☑ Rocks or paperweights

ALERT

Wet tea bags can cause stains. Handle with care.

To Do:

1. Place warm water into the bowl. Add tea bags and let them steep and cool for an hour.
2. Meanwhile, write this in ink on a piece of paper: "Roses are red. Violets are blue. I'm a supersecret agent and I'm going to find you."
3. Place the paper on a tray. Take a tea bag and gently rub it all over the paper. Repeat using the remaining tea bags. Be careful not to tear the paper.

4. Open one of the tea bags and spread the tea leaves over the paper.
5. If your paper is sopping wet, gently blot it using paper towels.
6. Use rocks to hold down the corners of the paper. Allow the paper to dry completely.
7. When dried, remove the paper from under the rock. Discard the tea leaves.

TRADE SECRETS REVEALED

Tea gets its staining power from **tannins**. This naturally occurring compound is found in tree bark, in the seeds and stems of grapes, and in tea leaves. Tannins give tea its flavor and rich brown color.

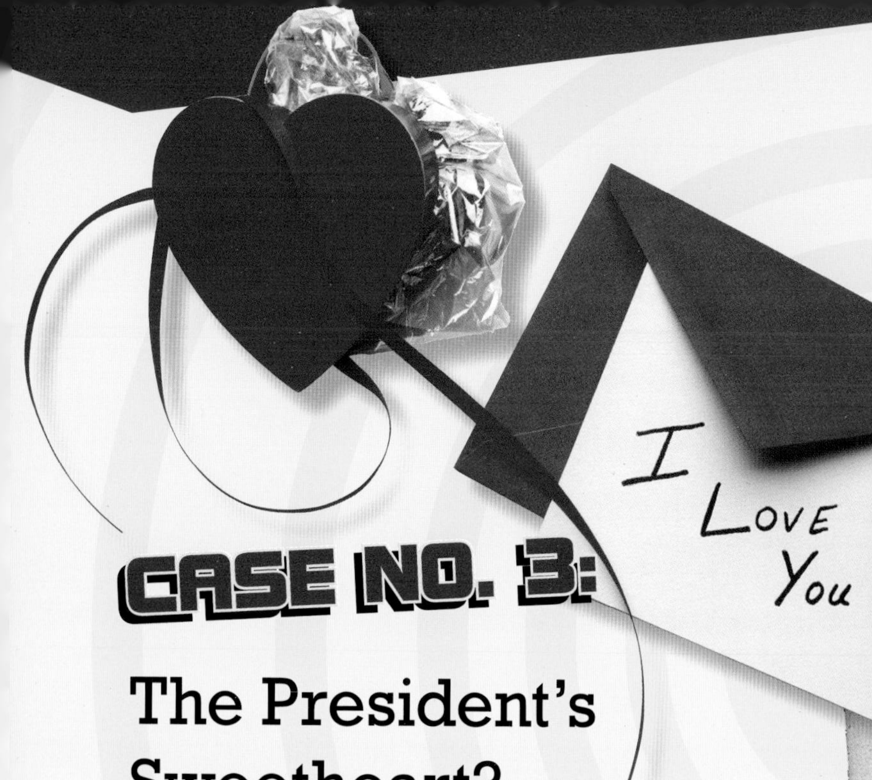

CASE NO. 3:

The President's Sweetheart?

Did a reporter uncover a great love story? Or was it a publicity stunt?

In 1928, Wilma Frances Minor, a columnist at a newspaper, claimed that she had found a bunch of love letters between a young Abraham Lincoln, long before he became the 16th president of the United States, and his supposed girlfriend, Ann Rutledge.

Minor contacted the editor of a magazine, and the editor eagerly paid the columnist a large sum to write a three-part series about her discovery. When the stories hit the newsstands, Lincoln scholars quickly raised red flags.

Important dates and events in Lincoln's life were inaccurate. Also, the handwriting in the published letters did not match the one found in genuine Lincoln articles. Turns out, Minor forged all the letters. Her career was ruined.

Famous Lefty
Abraham Lincoln (1809-1865) was left-handed. He was considered a talented writer.

FORGERY HALL OF SHAME

In 1794, a 19-year-old Englishman named William Henry Ireland claimed that he had discovered a previously unknown play written by the famous playwright William Shakespeare. News about the "lost" Shakespearean play generated heated debate about its authenticity. Plans were made to produce the play, titled *Vortigern and Rowena*. On opening night, the audience booed to express their opinion. The play closed after one performance. In 1805, Ireland confessed that he had forged the play.

William Shakespeare (1564–1616)

Training Exercise:
Handwriting Analysis

How do you tell if a piece of writing is genuine or forged? Try this exercise to find out.

You Need:

- ☑ 4 fellow agents
- ☑ Writing paper
- ☑ Pen
- ☑ 4 pieces of tracing paper
- ☑ Magnifier

To Do:

1. Ask your team to select a member to write this message on a piece of paper: "Abort mission. The dead drop is no longer safe. My cover has been blown." They must not reveal to you who the agent is.
2. Ask each of your fellow agents, including the one who wrote the message, to write the same message on a piece of tracing paper. Label each sheet with the name of the agent who wrote the note.
3. Place one agent's tracing paper over the original note. Use a magnifier to examine the details of the writing. One by one, repeat the examination using the other pieces of tracing paper.
4. The handwriting in which piece of tracing paper best matches the penmanship in the original note?

SECRET AGENT TIP

A "dead drop" is a prearranged location where agents leave information for each other to pick up. This is the opposite of a live drop, which is a location where agents meet in person to exchange information.

TRADE SECRETS REVEALED

No two people write alike. That's why forensic document examiners analyze handwriting to catch forgers. You can likely conclude who wrote the note by checking for similarities in the shape of the letters and the spacing between the words.

CASE NO. 4:
Bank Scam

A crook made millions by using fake checks.

In the 1960s, native New Yorker Robert Abagnale embraced a life of crime. His claim to fame was altering checks or creating fake ones, and then cashing them in.

Abagnale began swindling banks when he was just 16 years old. To avoid getting caught, he traveled from country to country. He also constantly invented and switched identities as a cover-up. He successfully impersonated a pilot, a teacher, a lawyer, and a doctor!

By the time Abagnale was 21 years old, he had made millions using forged checks, and he was wanted by police in 26 countries. The law eventually caught up with Abagnale, and he spent five years in jail.

After he was released, the ex-con decided that he could use his "gift" as a successful forger to help the right side of the law. Today, Abagnale owns a company that helps the government and private companies avoid being scammed by check forgers.

TRADE SECRETS FROM THE HIDDEN FILES

Shhh

To help stop forgers, some pen companies have created special inks that can't be altered by chemicals or a solvent. When used, the super ink becomes "trapped" in paper fibers, making it impossible for crooks to alter checks and make off with someone else's cash.

Training Exercise: Fake Out

How can you tell if a document has been altered? Practice this crime-busting method with a fellow agent.

You Need:

- ☑ Fellow agent
- ☑ Pen
- ☑ Sheet of plain white paper
- ☑ Ink eraser
- ☑ Photocopier
- ☑ Magnifier

To Do:

1. On a sheet of white paper write the following: "The glee club will meet on Monday at 3 p.m."
2. Use an ink eraser to erase the word "Monday" and replace it with "Friday."
3. Make a photocopy of the document. Then give it and the magnifier to a fellow agent.
4. See if the agent can sleuth out what was altered in the document.

TRADE SECRETS REVEALED

When you use an eraser to alter a document, **friction** wears down the fibers in the paper. If you hunt for variations in the paper, you'll likely zero in on where the document had been altered.

CASE NO. 5:

Word Hunt

Savvy agents use puzzling ways to transmit top secret messages.

During World War II, German secret agents hid messages in a microdot, a piece of film as tiny as the period at the end of this sentence.

An agent would photograph a note, shrink the film to the size of a dot, and attach it to a period in a typewritten letter. The letter's recipient would hunt for the dot, remove it, and read the message contained in the dot using a microscope.

Besides microdots, **codes** and **ciphers** are other great ways to disguise your messages. Even if your note gets intercepted, the thief would have a hard time making sense of the mumbo jumbo.

SECRET AGENT TIP

Learn agent lingo! A communiqué is an official report.

Training Exercise: Cryptology

There are many ways to encrypt messages. You are about to learn one of the most famous methods.

You Need:

- ☑ Paper
- ☑ Pencil

To Do:

1. Write down a word that doesn't have any letters repeated in it. For example: "agent."
2. Following the word, write the alphabet in order from A to Z, minus the letters that appear in your chosen word. It should look something like this:

A G E N T B C D F H I J K L M O P Q R S U V W X Y Z

Shhh

TRADE SECRETS FROM THE HIDDEN FILES

Julius Caesar was a powerful political and military leader in ancient Rome. He used a cipher to protect the messages he sent to his most trusted associates. Caesar shifted each letter in the early Roman alphabet by three positions. For example, "A" becomes "D," and "B" becomes "E."

3. Under the letters, write the alphabet from A to Z.

   See below:

A G E N T B C D F H I J K L M O P Q R S U V W X Y Z
A B C D E F G H I J K L M N O P Q R S T U V W X Y Z

4. Each letter in the top line now replaces the corresponding letter below. Use the key above to decode the following message.

EMLCQASUJASFMLR. YMU DAVT RUEETRRBUJJY EMKOJTSTN YMUQ EQYOSMJMCY SQAFLFLC.

To find the answer, turn this page upside down.

SECRET AGENT HALL OF FAME

During World Wars I and II, the military often used homing pigeons to deliver coded messages. The specially trained birds wore unbreakable canisters to carry the notes. Some of the birds also wore cameras to snap images above enemy lines!

Answer: Congratulations. You have successfully completed your cryptology training.

Training Exercise: Graphology

Do you have the personality to be a supersecret agent? Some people think that they can tell just by studying your handwriting. Graphologists believe that a person's behavior and sense of self-esteem is expressed through his or her penmanship.

Graphology is not a science. Some people take it seriously, but others don't. Do you believe in it? Let's study the handwriting of your fellow agents and see.

You Need:

- ☑ Fellow agents
- ☑ Unlined paper
- ☑ Pens

To Do:

1. Have each member of your team write the following sentence on a piece of paper:
   "The quick brown fox jumps over the lazy dog."
2. Use the guide on the following pages to analyze the handwriting samples. Does the agent's penmanship match her personality?

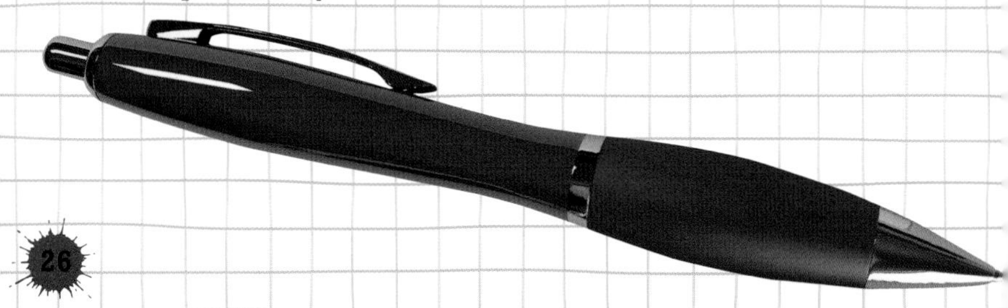

TRADE SECRETS FROM THE HIDDEN FILES

Shhh

In 1885, the *Michigan School Moderator*, a journal for educators, advised teachers to use the sentence "The quick brown fox jumps over the lazy dog" to help kids practice their penmanship. Why? The sentence is a **pangram**; it includes all the letters in the English alphabet. The phrase became very popular throughout the 20th century. People used it to perfect their typing skills. Today, the phrase is often used to test computer keyboards.

GRAPHOLOGY GUIDE

Which way does your writing slant?

Right: You have a very strong emotional response to people and circumstances. right

Straight up and down: You are restrained. Straight

Mixed: You are sensitive and unpredictable. Mixed

Left: You keep your emotions hidden. 

Where do you cross your "t"s?

Very high: You're reaching for the stars.

3/4 of the way up: You're realistic about your goals.

Very low: Challenging yourself is not a priority.

What does your personal pronoun "I" look like?

Well-balanced in cursive, with both an upper loop and a lower hook: You probably have a good relationship with your superiors.

A stick figure, written with a single stroke: You're independent. 

Printed, not in cursive: You are independent, too.

Very large: You're confident and take up a lot of personal space.

Very small: You don't like to draw a lot of attention to yourself.

How do you dot your "i"s?

High over the stem: Your thoughts are high in the sky.

Missing completely: You have trouble remembering things that you're supposed to finish.

Close to the stem: You're very detailed. i

With a circle: You need a lot of attention. i

How do you make capital letters?

Large: You're extremely self-confident. Large

Small: You prefer to blend in with the crowd. Small

Fancy: You're a show-off. Fancy

How crowded is your writing?

Crowded: You may be shy and withdrawn. crowded

Takes up the whole page: You have a lot of confidence. whole page

How big are your letters?

Small and neat: You are very focused and controlled. small and neat

Huge: Chances are you're loose and carefree. You find it hard to concentrate. huge

Evenly sized: You're very reliable. perfect

How much pressure do you use to write?

Heavy: You're committed to whatever task you take on; you take things seriously. Heavy

Light: You're sensitive to other people's feelings. light

MISSION ACCOMPLISHED

WELL DONE, SUPERSECRET AGENT!

You have completed your training mission.

You have proven that you have the wits and smarts for undercover work. But there's much more training ahead.

The tips below will help you move on to the next level, which is critical if you ever want to become a pro.

1. Crack those books! You need a college degree with a high GPA in order to become a secret agent for government agencies like the FBI or the CIA. Some positions require advanced degrees.
2. Take courses in math, science (behavioral, physical, and computer), engineering, economics, international relations, and technology. Brainiacs are awesome!
3. Master a foreign language—or two or three. Secret agents are sent all over the world at a drop of a hat. You must be able to speak like a native if you don't want to blow your cover.

4. Have excellent communication skills. You need to be in touch with your secret agent network at all times.

5. Be physically fit. Running away from, or after, criminals is exhausting.

6. You must be able to keep a secret! If you feel the need to share everything with your BFF, secret agent work is not for you.

SECRET AGENT HALL OF FAME

From 1992 to 1996, Stella Rimington served as the first female head of MI5, the United Kingdom's Secret Service.

Girls Rule!

More than 2,000 women serve as FBI Special Agents. Many of them are in high-profile leadership positions.

GLOSSARY

Acid: Liquid that is usually characterized as having a sour taste. Acid contains an excess of hydrogen ions, or electrically charged particles.

Chromatogram: Pattern of separated substances obtained through chromatography

Chromatography: Chemical technique that separates mixtures

Cipher: System of secret writing that involves letters jumbled up or replaced by other letters, numbers, or symbols

Code: System of secret communication that involves entire words or phrases replaced by other words, phrases, or numbers

Forensic: Using science to gather evidence that could help in the investigation of crimes

Friction: Rubbing force

Oxidize: To combine with oxygen and chemically change

Pangram: Sentence incorporating all the letters of the alphabet

Pigment: Substance used as coloring

Porous: Full of pores that can be penetrated

Soluble: Capable of being dissolved in a solvent

Solvent: Usually a liquid substance that can dissolve another substance

Tannin: Chemical compound in tea that provides flavor and color